Creatures and Characters

OTHER SCHIFFER BOOKS BY TIMOTHY YOUNG:

Am I Big Enough? A Fun Little Book on Manners, ISBN 978-0-7643-5053-5

The Angry Little Puffin, ISBN 978-0-7643-4805-1

Do Not Open the Box! ISBN 978-0-7643-5043-6

Copyright © 2017 by Timothy Young

Library of Congress Control Number: 2017935422

All rights reserved. No part of this work may be reproduced or used in any form or by any means—graphic, electronic, or mechanical, including photocopying or information storage and retrieval systems—without written permission from the publisher.

The scanning, uploading, and distribution of this book or any part thereof via the Internet or any other means without the permission of the publisher is illegal and punishable by law. Please purchase only authorized editions and do not participate in or encourage the electronic piracy of copyrighted materials.

"Schiffer," "Schiffer Publishing, Ltd.," and the pen and inkwell logo are registered trademarks of Schiffer Publishing, Ltd.

Cover design by Brenda McCallum
Type set in Kidprint MT Std

ISBN: 978-0-7643-5403-8
Printed in China

Published by Schiffer Publishing, Ltd.
4880 Lower Valley Road
Atglen, PA 19310
Phone: (610) 593-1777; Fax: (610) 593-2002
E-mail: Info@schifferbooks.com
Web: www.schifferbooks.com

For our complete selection of fine books on this and related subjects, please visit our website at www.schifferbooks.com. You may also write for a free catalog.

Schiffer Publishing's titles are available at special discounts for bulk purchases for sales promotions or premiums. Special editions, including personalized covers, corporate imprints, and excerpts, can be created in large quantities for special needs. For more information, contact the publisher.

We are always looking for people to write books on new and related subjects. If you have an idea for a book, please contact us at proposals@schifferbooks.com.

CREATURES AND CHARACTERS

Drawing Amazing Monsters, Aliens, and Other Weird Things!

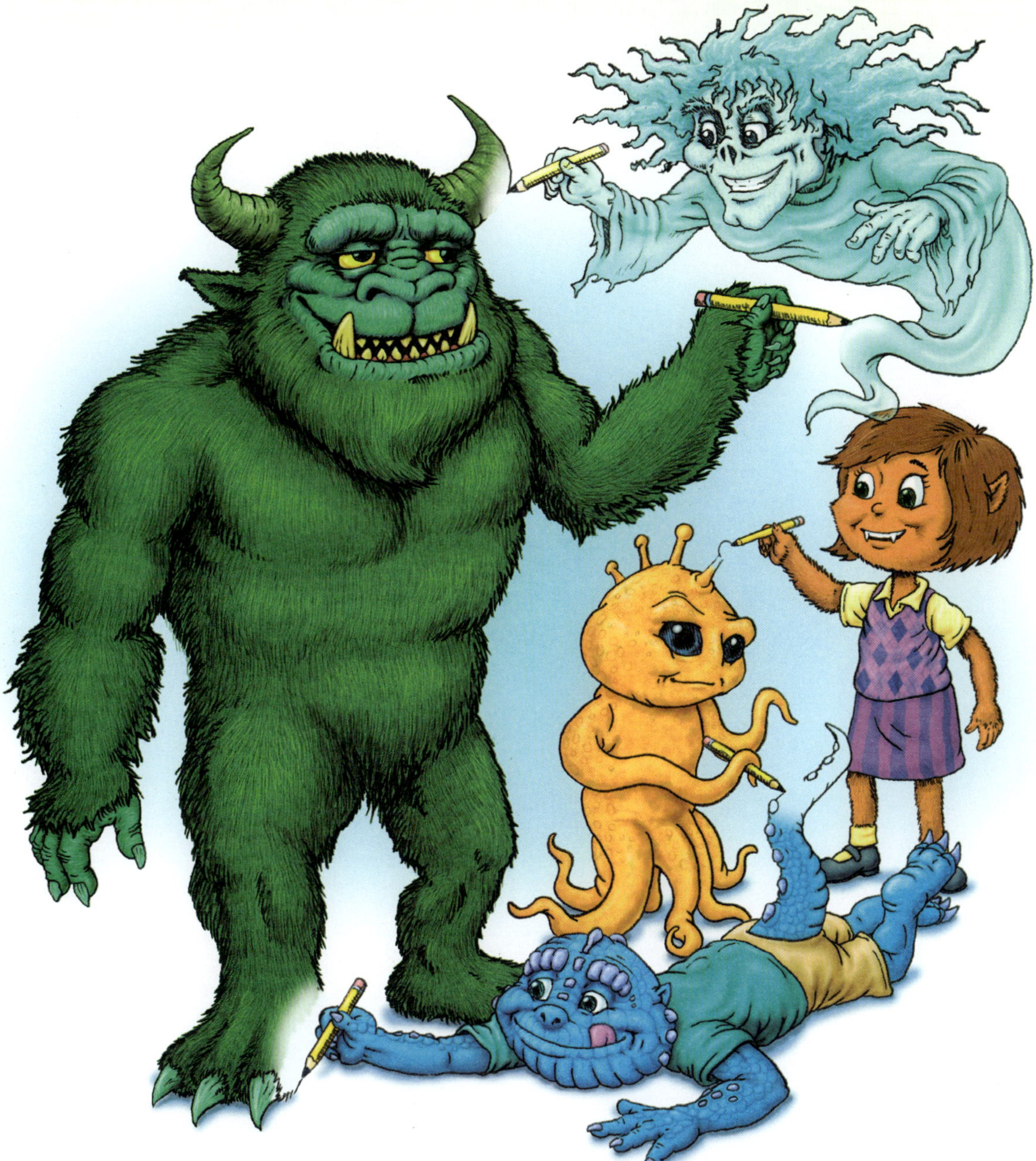

TIMOTHY YOUNG

4880 Lower Valley Road • Atglen, PA 19310

Introduction

Ever since I was a little kid I've loved drawing aliens, dinosaurs, animals, monsters—all kinds of creatures and characters! I watched a lot of monster movies and read a lot of science fiction stories. Then I drew the things I liked from those and made up all kinds of other ones.

Many of the books I've published have monsters and aliens in them. When I visit schools, students, teachers, and librarians ask me how I come up with these weird, funny, strange, and silly creatures and characters. So I decided to put this book together to show how you how to draw and be creative.

If I've visited your school or library you'll have seen my "scribble drawing" presentation. That's in here, along with other fun techniques you can try.

Character designers work in many fields. Artists design characters for movies, television shows, video games, toys, books, and comics. The characters on this page come from a few different book ideas. They show how you can use many styles to draw your creations.

Creature and Character Design

Creating new creatures and characters from your imagination is really fun. When creating new creatures, whether they are monsters, aliens, or some new, bizarre thing, you can set the rules and decide what they are, where they come from, and what they look like.

These are some creature and character-based toys that I created while working in the toy industry.

ART SUPPLIES

How many tools do you need to draw? Not a whole lot, really. This is my drawing table and these are some of the art supplies I used to draw the creatures and characters in this book.

Pencils, crayons, pens, markers, and paper are the basic tools for drawing. Everything else is just extra. Some tools, like rulers and squares, can help you draw straighter lines. For paper, carry a sketchbook and a few markers and pencils so you can draw wherever you go. You can also draw on inexpensive printer or copy paper from any store. Expensive art supplies can be fun to use, but you don't need stuff that costs a lot to draw cool pictures.

The only really pricey thing in this picture is the lightbox. A lightbox is great for tracing your drawings onto thicker paper. The light comes through and shows the drawing on the paper underneath. The best lightboxes are made with LEDs and Plexiglas. They are lightweight and they don't get hot so you can draw anywhere, even on your lap. You can find small ones for less than $40. Ask for one for your birthday.

You can also draw on really cheap tracing paper. Pads of tracing paper in the stationary section of your local supermarket cost $3 or less a pad, and it's better than the expensive tracing paper from an art supply store.

The one tool I use in my illustrations that is not in this picture is a computer. After I make a drawing I scan it into my computer and finish it in Adobe Photoshop. This book shows a lot of finished illustrations, but just remember that all the original drawings were done with the tools shown here.

PENCIL VS INK

Is it better to draw in pencil or ink? It depends on how you want your drawing to look and which medium you prefer.

Pencil gives you a softer line and you can get very subtle shading.

One of my favorite movies is the original black and white *King Kong*. I love when he battles the Tyrannosaurus Rex!

Depending on the type of pencil you use, you can erase any mistakes.

Ink, whether from a pen or a marker, gives you a crisp, dark line. The contrast between black and white is more distinct.

If you use a waterproof marker, you can then color your drawing with marker or watercolor paint. This is harder to do over pencil.

A problem with ink is that mistakes are harder to fix. Ink erasers don't work well, but you can use correction fluid or white paint to hide the mistake.

To make shadows with ink, you can use drawing techniques like crosshatching, using many thin lines to give the effect of darker areas.

Doodles, Sketches & Scribbles

What's the difference?

Doodles:

Many people use the words doodle, sketch, and scribble interchangeably when describing a rough drawing, but they are very different. A doodle is a drawing that you just start doing and you have no idea how it's going to end up until you are finished. All of the creatures on this page are doodles drawn with a fine point marker.

You can start by drawing the head, or start with the eyes or the teeth. Get a pencil or marker and see where your hand and imagination take you.

Sometimes you might not want to draw the bodies, only the heads.

Doodles, Sketches & Scribbles

Sketches:

Sketches are rougher drawings. When you sketch, you usually have an idea of what you're trying to draw, and you want to get a basic drawing of the character you're thinking about.

Lightly draw some simple shapes first and then go over those lines with darker, more precise lines.

Don't worry if there are extra lines showing through since these are not final drawings.

Here are some more sketches.

Small, quick sketches are called thumbnails. They are often used to work out poses or scenes from a story.

Some artists like to sketch using colored pencil. Comic book artists and animators often use blue pencil and then ink over top of the blue lines.

Using your thumbnail sketches, you can do more detailed sketches of your character. Sketching is useful as a way to develop the same character in different poses.

Doodles, Sketches & Scribbles

When sketching a new character, you might be looking for a body type before you know what kind of final character you want.

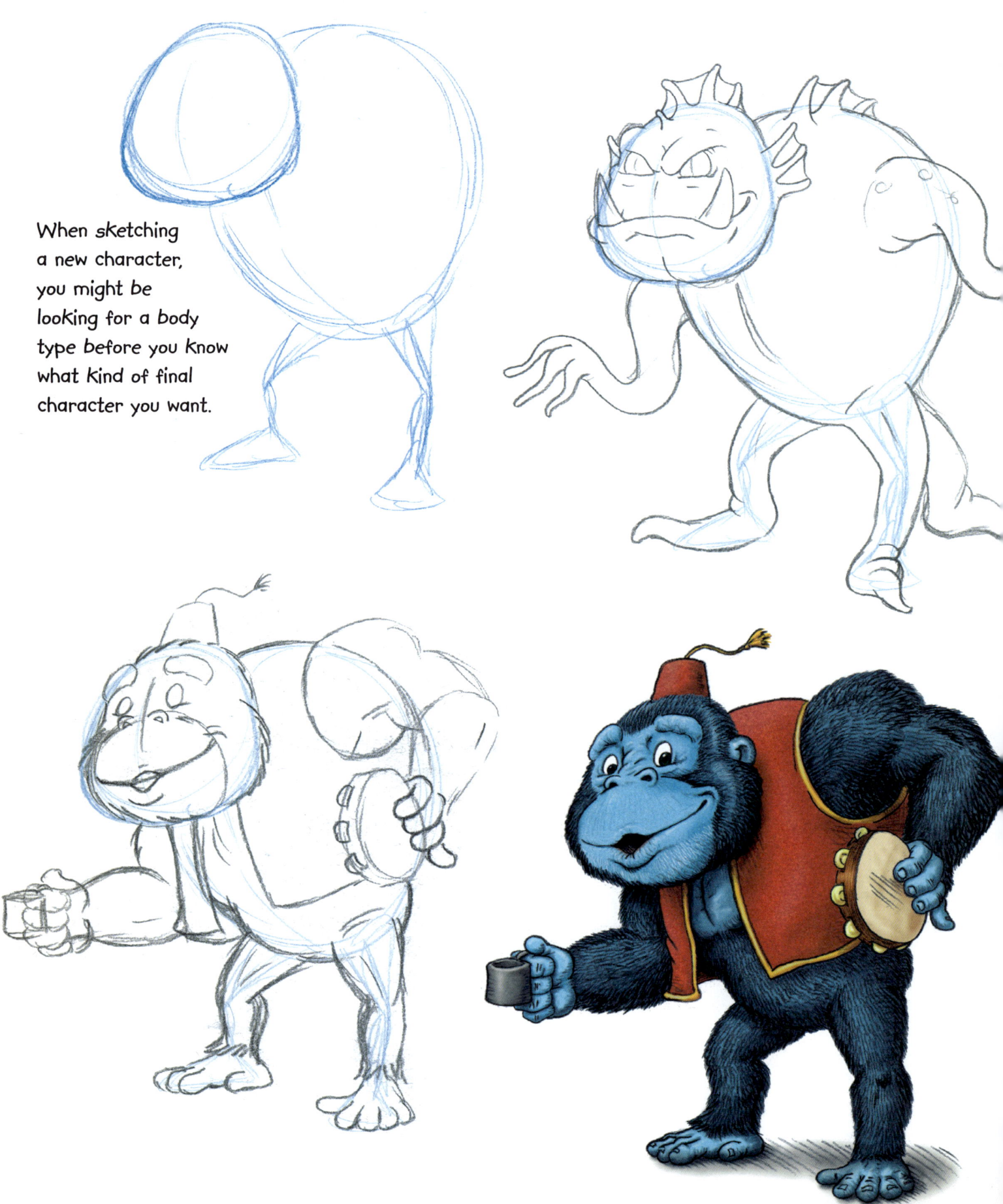

Here are three different characters drawn from the same initial sketch. This is where using tracing paper or a lightbox can come in handy. You can trace over the same rough sketch over and over.

As you've noticed by now, this is not one of those "draw three circles and then finish it into a Viking" book. While those books are great, this book is about using your imagination to come up with your very own characters. If you want to draw these characters, please do so, but also try to come up with unique characters of your own.

Doodles, Sketches & Scribbles

Scribbles:

Scribble drawings are a lot of fun and are a great way to spark creativity. First make a random scribble. You don't even have to look at the paper; just let your hand go where it wants.

Then look at the scribble and find a character hidden in the scribble.

Try using a colored marker or pencil to do the scribble, then draw your character in black.

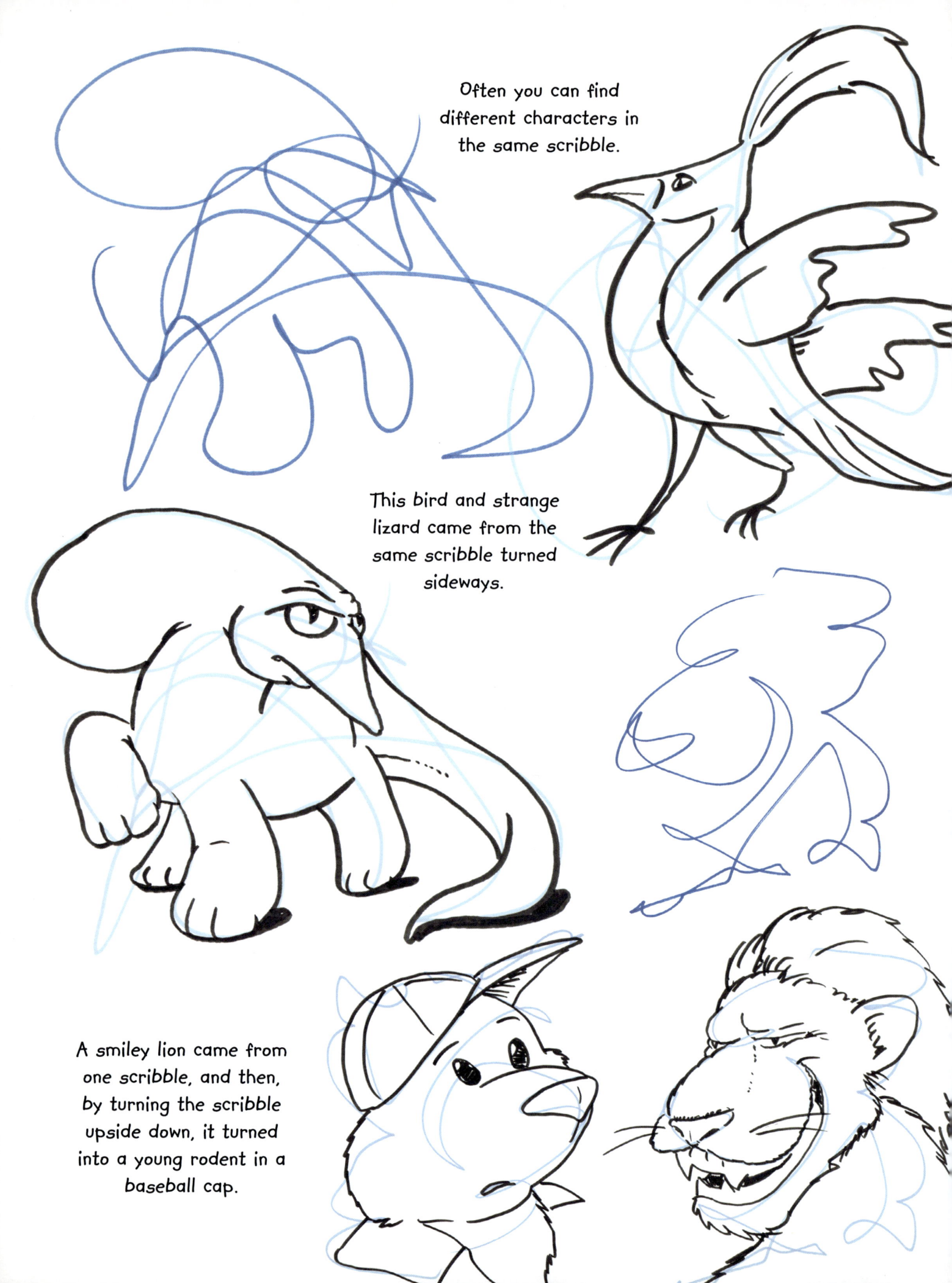

This scribble was hiding these three different characters.

Once you've practiced seeing creatures and characters in scribbles, you might just start seeing them everywhere. Almost everyone has looked at clouds and seen bunnies or elephants. There's even a scientific term for seeing faces or other things in the random patterns of other objects. It's called pareidolia.

From our ancient ancestors who painted animals on the walls of caves, to Leonardo da Vinci, many artists have used this technique to inspire their art.

If you open your eyes and let your imagination go, you can see almost anything in the shapes and patterns around you.

CREATING CREATURES:
Classic Monsters

Classic Monsters are a great place to start for inspiration when creating your own characters. From ghosts and witches and zombies to Dracula, Frankenstein, and Wolfman, there are so many to choose from. The great thing for an illustrator is that there are many ways you can interpret these creatures. You can make detailed, frightening versions, or cute and funny drawings.
Play, have fun, and be creative!

CREATING CREATURES: MYTHOLOGICAL MONSTERS

Another way to create new creatures is to combine people and animals together. People have created monsters since ancient times; stories of vampires, werewolves, and zombies go back centuries. The Mediterranean cultures combined animals to create unique monsters. Here are some of them.

Capricorn, the sea-goat, had the front half of a goat and the tail of a fish.

A sphinx had the head of a man or woman, the wings of an eagle, and the body of a lion. Many mythical monsters had lion parts.

The manticore had a man's head and a large mouth with three rows of teeth. It also had the body of a lion (a red one), the wings of a bat, and a long, spike-covered tail.

The strangest mythological creature was the chimera, which had the head and front legs of a lion, and the head and back legs of a goat. Its tail was a snake. The head of the goat came out of its back.

CREATING CREATURES: NEW MYTHICAL BEASTS

It's fun to make your own mythical monsters by combining different animals. Take two or three animals you like and turn them into a brand new creature.

Here's one with the head of an elephant, the body of a bear, and the tail of an alligator.

Let's call it an eligatear.

This one is part wolf and part octopus, and it has bat wings.

Let's call it a watopus.

Here's one with the head and fin of a shark, the back legs and tail of a rooster, and the mane and front legs of a lion.
(You must have one with lion parts, after all.)

What would you name this one?

CREATING CREATURES: MONSTERS & ALIENS
What are the differences?

The biggest difference between monsters and aliens is that aliens come from space and monsters are from Earth. Unless, of course, it's an alien monster from outer space.

Unlike aliens, monsters are hairy . . . or scaly, or slimy, or maybe even covered in feathers. They are green or brown or red or maybe purple or blue.

Another difference is in the weapons it might use. If it has a raygun it's probably an alien, whereas a monster would carry a club or a big rock. Unless it's a primitive alien carrying a club, or a monster created in a lab in the future and it grabs a raygun.

Unlike monsters, aliens are slimy . . . or scaly or hairy or maybe even covered in feathers. They are green or brown or red or maybe purple or blue. Wait, this sounds familiar . . . did I say this already?

Okay, never mind, there really is no difference when you are creating monsters and aliens. There are no rules. If you say it's a monster, it's a monster. If you are designing aliens, they're aliens. It's entirely up to you!

Okay, I've got it—monsters don't wear clothes and aliens do.

Wait, Dracula and Frankenstein wear clothes and E. T. doesn't. Aaarghh!!

MONSTERS or ALIENS? You Decide!

CREATING CREATURES: Developing Characters

The next couple of pages show the development of two aliens. This page shows the original designs.

An earlier version of this grumpy guy with the big brain (right) can be seen in the beginning of this book.

Let's call him Brainy.

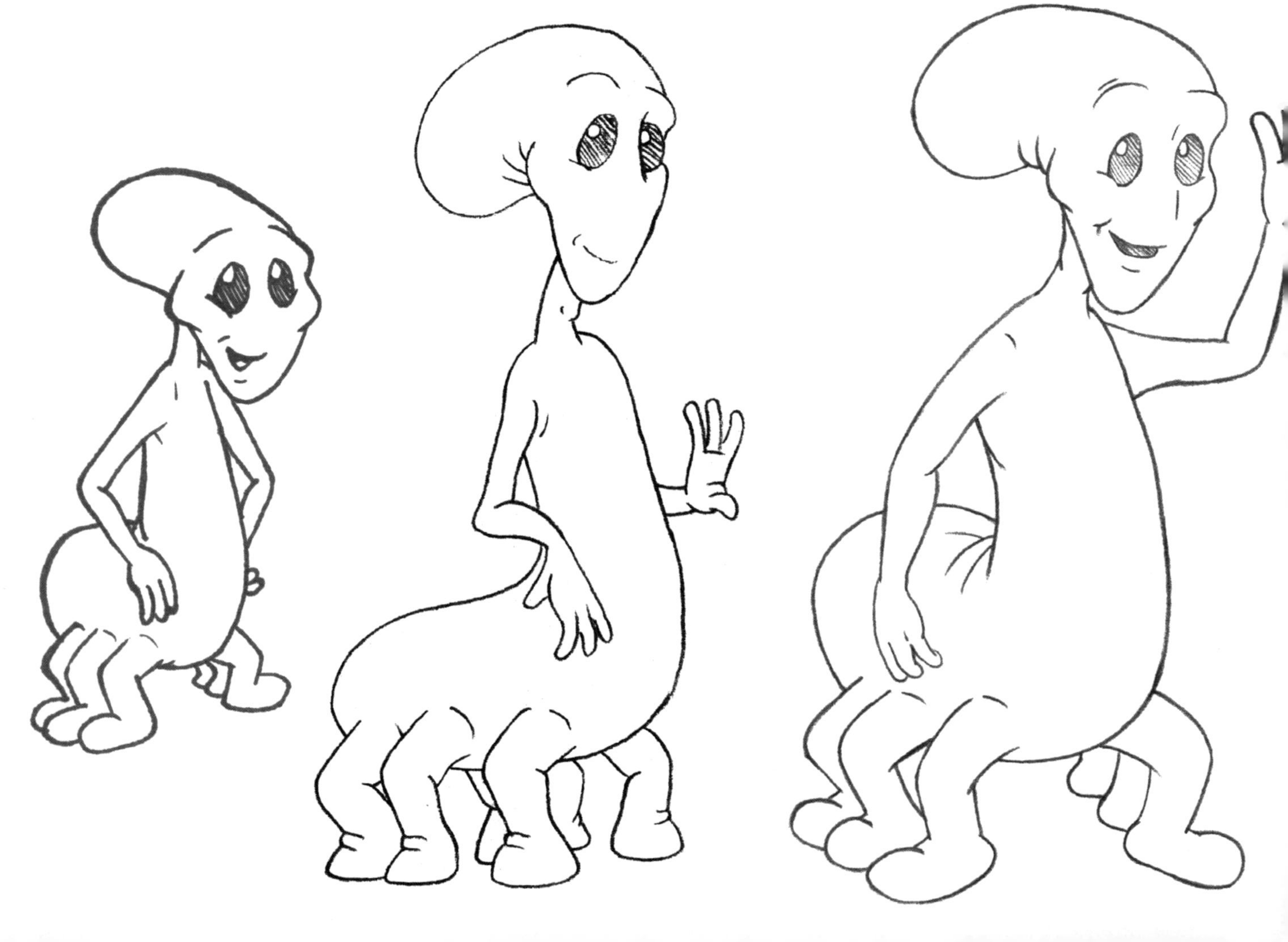

CREATING CREATURES: Coloring and Rendering Characters

Once you've designed your characters, you have to decide how you want to color and render them. You can choose to keep things simple like the ones below with flat colors for highlights and shadows.

This coloring and rendering was done with Photoshop, but you can get similar effects with traditional art supplies.

For flat colors you can use markers or acrylic or gouache paints.

On the next two versions on this page I used more subtle shading. Lumpy has subtler shading than Brainy. You can use markers or colored pencils to do this kind of lightening and shading.

Play around with skin texturing as well as coloring. Under his spots Lumpy has another circle pattern on his skin.

The set above shows Lumpy and Brainy without their outlines. Many illustrators only use line-work in their sketches and then eliminate them when they do their finished illustration.

Look at different picture books and illustrations. There are so many techniques for creating and rendering characters. Find your favorite ways to work, using the materials you enjoy working with.

Sometimes illustrators or character designers have to work with another artist's characters. If you are designing a toy based on a cartoon or book character, you have to draw them in the correct style.

Seussified

Tracing characters from a book you like is a great way to understand how the original was drawn. It's a great way to learn to draw.

There are so many resources for finding out about your favorite artists and how they create their work. If you like a certain style of illustration, such as watercolors or collage, find out how it's done and give it a try.

SENDAKIAN

It's fun to try to figure out how your favorite illustrators would draw your characters, too. These samples are rendered in the style of three popular picture book illustrators. Who are your favorites?

CARLE-ISH

Silhouettes

Silhouettes are made by drawing a figure as a dark shape against a bright background. The illustration on the left shows a monster lit from behind by the moon. You can also use silhouettes to create a more graphic look like the samples here, using a bold color background.

Try drawing your creature first and then figuring out the outlines. You can bring out the teeth, eyes, and claws with white and add color highlights to show some of the body structure (these are the lines that use the background color).

Random Creatures & Characters

The next couple of pages illustrate random creatures and characters that may inspire you to create your own. This page has some fun and funky guys.

These are creepier beasties, things with nasty claws and sharp fangs.

Now it's your turn to create new creatures and characters! Whether they're hairy or scaly or covered in slime, have fun making your own monsters, aliens, and other weird things!

About the Author

Timothy Young has been drawing monsters, aliens, and all kinds of weird creatures for most of his life. He drew them at home lying on the living room rug while watching television and at school on his homework and test papers. He wondered who made the cartoons and books he liked and who got to make the toys he played with. Little did he know that he would one day get to do those things.

As he got older, he got better at drawing. He went to Pratt Institute in Brooklyn, New York, where he studied illustration and sculpting. Soon after college he got his first job designing and sculpting animation models for the television show *Pee-Wee's Playhouse*. Other highlights of his career were working for the Muppets and being the design director for two toy companies. After a fun career designing creatures and characters for animation, toys, and illustrations, he now writes and illustrates picture books.

If you would like to learn more about Tim and see videos of him drawing some of the creatures and characters in this book, visit his website at www.CreaturesAndCharacters.com.